A place to:

serve

RYLAND WALTER

SENIOR PASTOR, ROCK BROOK CHURCH

conversation series

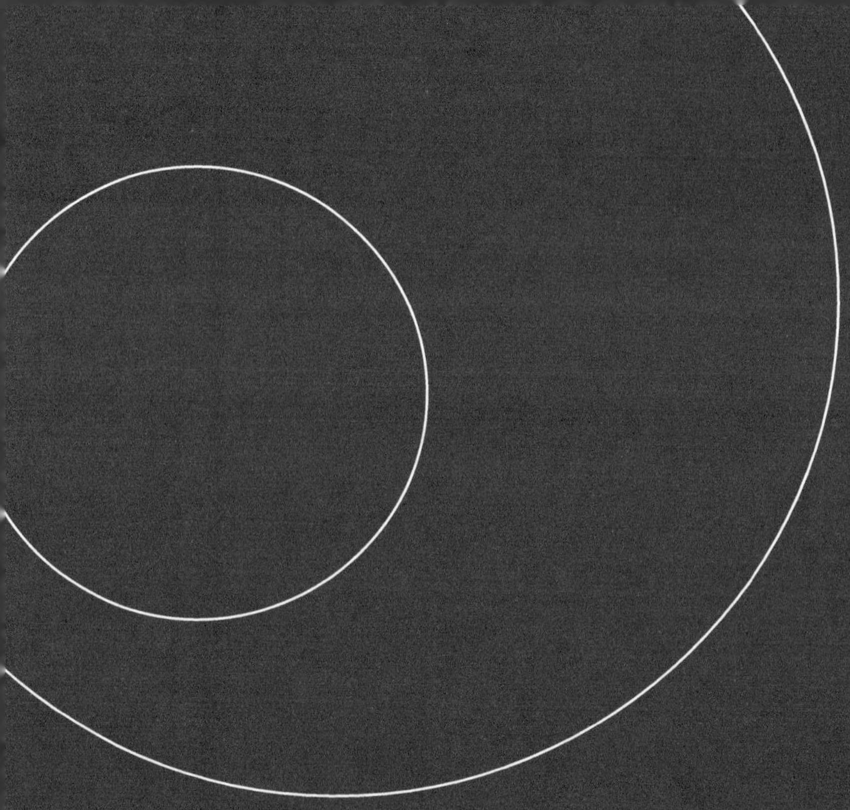

Published by LifeTogether.

ISBN: 978-1-7322325-4-9
Printed in the United States of America

contents

SESSIONS

APPENDICES

SMALL GROUP LEADERS

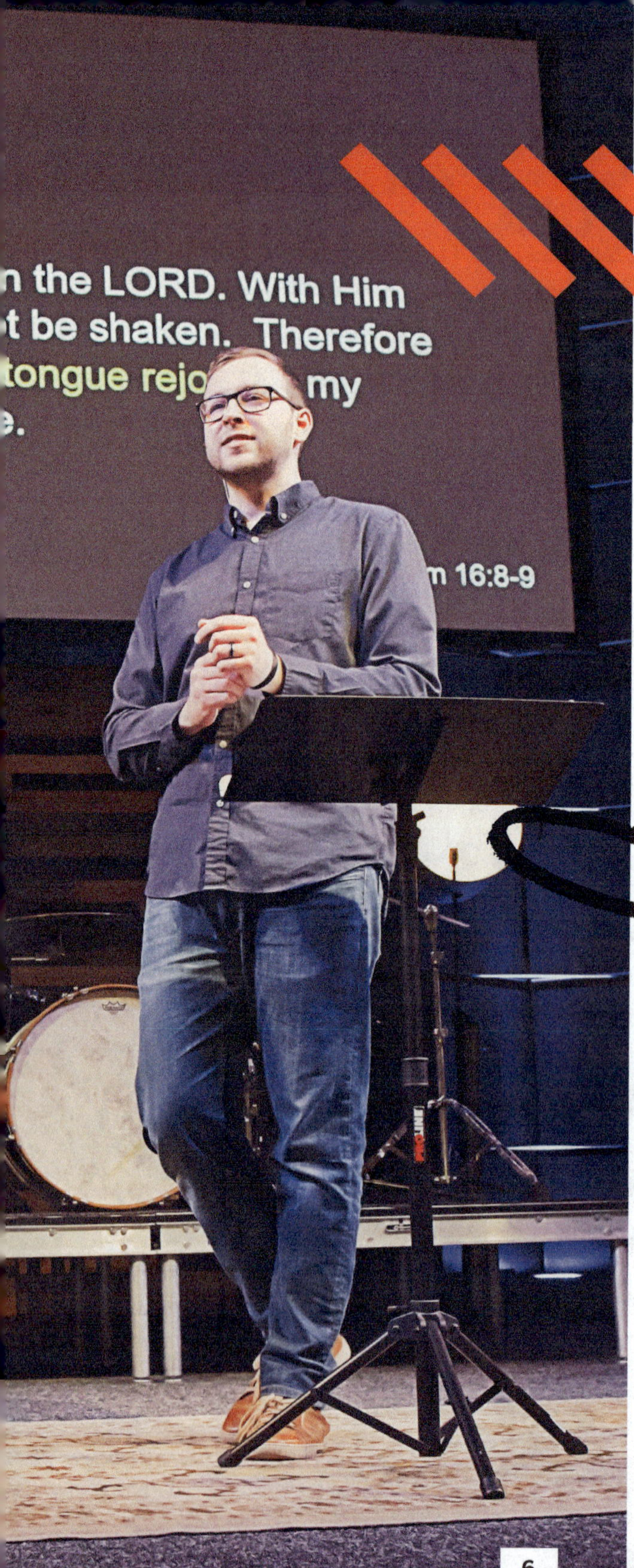
n the LORD. With Him
t be shaken. Therefore
tongue rejo my
e.
m 16:8-9

welcome

Here at Rock Brook we have a saying: Come As You Are! We really mean that and want to give you a warm welcome. No matter where you find yourself in life, you belong here.

Jesus is our model for a life of service. Jesus knew what His mission was and what His identity was, and what His calling was, and so He could humble himself and serve others.

We serve out of the overflow of who we are, and we serve because we know who we are in Christ. If Jesus, through whom the universe was created and through whom we are saved, can serve us, how much more can we learn to serve each other!

This understanding of God's heart to serve is the foundation of our own heart to serve. In the coming weeks we will discover more of what it means to serve others, and how this is not only something we "should" do as followers of Jesus, but a privilege that can give us joy.

Whether you are new to Rock Brook or long-time family, we are praying for you. We believe that through this tool you will truly be encouraged, loved, and your life will be genuinely transformed!

Ryland Walter

RYLAND WALTER

SENIOR PASTOR, ROCK BROOK CHURCH

using THIS WORKBOOK

1. Notice in the Table of Contents there are three sections: (1) Sessions; (2) Appendices; and (3) Small Group Leaders. Familiarize yourself with the Appendices. Some of them will be used in the sessions themselves.

2. If you are leading or co-leading a small group, the section Small Group Leaders will give you tips for effective leadership, encourage you, and help you avoid a few common obstacles.

3. Use this workbook as a guide. If the group responds to the lesson in an unexpected but honest way, go with that. If you think of a better question than the next one in the lesson, ask it. Take to heart the insights included in the Frequently Asked Questions pages and the Small Group Leaders section.

4. Enjoy your Small Group experience.

5. Pray before each session—for your group members, for your time together and for wisdom and insight.

6. Read the Outline of Each Session on the next pages so you understand how the sessions will flow.

outline OF EACH SESSION

A typical group session for the Serve study will include the following sections. Read through this to get a clear idea of how each group meeting will be structured:

WEEKLY MEMORY VERSES. Each session opens with a memory verse that emphasizes an important truth from the session. This is an optional exercise, but we believe memorizing scripture is a powerful way to grow spiritually. We encourage you to give this important habit a try. The verses for each session are also listed in the appendix.

INTRODUCTION. Each lesson opens with a brief thought that will help you prepare for the session and get you thinking about that week's topic. Make it a practice to read these before the session. You may want to have the group read them aloud.

SHARE YOUR STORY. The foundation for spiritual growth is an intimate connection with God and His family. You build that connection by sharing your story with a few people who really know. This section includes some simple questions to get you talking—letting you share as much or as little of your story as you choose.

HEAR GOD'S STORY. In this section, you'll read the Bible and listen to a teaching in order to hear God's story—and begin to see how His story aligns with yours. When the study directs you to, you'll watch a short teaching segment on video. You'll then have an opportunity to read a passage of scripture and discuss both the teaching and the text. The goal isn't to accumulate information, but to apply the insights from scripture to your daily life.

CREATE A NEW STORY. In this section, you'll have an opportunity to go beyond Bible study to biblical living. This section will also have a question or two that will challenge you to live out your faith by serving others, sharing your faith, or worshiping God.

DAILY DEVOTIONS. Each week on the daily devotions pages, we provide scriptures to reflect on between sessions. This provides you with a chance to slow down, read just a small portion of scripture each day, and pray through it. You'll then have a chance to journal your thoughts about what you just read. Use this section to seek God on your own throughout the week. This time at home should begin and end with prayer. Don't get in a hurry; take enough time to hear from God and talk to him!

SESSION ONE

Discover God's Heart To Serve

"...whoever wants to become great among you must be your servant, and whoever wants to be first must be your slave— just as the Son of Man did not come to be served, but to serve, and to give his life as a ransom for many."

Matthew 20:26-28

If you've ever experienced exceptional service—perhaps at a hotel, fancy restaurant, or upscale retail establishment—you know how great it can feel to be served. Attentive service makes us feel appreciated, honored, and respected.

It is wonderful to be served, but God invites us to discover the unexpected joy of serving others. When we serve, we are not only following the example of Jesus—we're growing closer to him in the process. Serving strengthens the bonds between us and God, and also the bonds of our community with others.

leader notes

- If your group is new, welcome newcomers. Introduce everyone—you may even want to have name tags for your first meeting.
- Open your group with a brief prayer asking for insight as you study. You can pray for specific requests at the end of the meeting, or stop momentarily to pray if a particular situation comes up during your discussion.

YOUR STORY

Begin your time together by using the following questions to get the conversation started.

- Take a few minutes for each person to share their spiritual story. Did you grow up in church, or did you start exploring faith as an adult?
- On a scale of 1 to 10, how much of your time and energy is directed to your spiritual life in this season?
- What are you hoping to get out of this group?

watch THE VIDEO

Use the Notes space provided below to record your thoughts and questions as well as the things you want to remember or follow up on. After watching the video, have someone read the discussion questions in the Hear God's Story section and start the conversation.

hear

GOD'S STORY

Read John 13:1-5

"It was just before the Passover Festival. Jesus knew that the hour had come for him to leave this world and go to the Father. Having loved his own who were in the world, he loved them to the end. The evening meal was in progress, and the devil had already prompted Judas, the son of Simon Iscariot, to betray Jesus. Jesus knew that the Father had put all things under his power, and that he had come from God and was returning to God; so he got up from the meal, took off his outer clothing, and wrapped a towel around his waist. After that, he poured water into a basin and began to wash his disciples' feet, drying them with the towel that was wrapped around him."

- This passage says, "Jesus knew..." What did he know? What thoughts and feelings do you think Jesus experienced, knowing what He did?
- Why do you think Jesus chose to wash His disciples' feet? What was He trying to teach them?
- The text says that Judas had already decided to betray Jesus. But Judas was at the table. Imagine yourself in Judas' place, looking into Jesus' eyes as he washes your feet. What goes through your mind?

A NEW STORY

In this section, talk about how you will apply the wisdom you've learned from the teaching. Then think about practical steps you can take in the coming week to live out what you've learned.

- In our culture, we typically don't wash feet before a meal. However, we're called to serve as Jesus did. What's a specific way that you might serve someone this week?
- The passage we read describes Jesus' love for his disciples. He has this same kind of deep love for you. What feelings or thoughts does this love stir in you?
- Jesus put his love for his disciples into action. What's one way you can put your love for others into action this week? Be as specific as you can.

Give each person an opportunity to share prayer requests. If you'd like, you can write these on the Prayer and Praise Report on page 82.

Close your meeting with prayer.

Day 1

Galatians 5:13

"You, my brothers and sisters, were called to be free. But do not use your freedom to indulge the flesh; rather, serve one another humbly in love."

Reflect:

How can you use your freedom to serve others? What does it look like to serve humbly?

Day 2

Matthew 25:40

"The King will reply, 'Truly I tell you, whatever you did for one of the least of these brothers and sisters of mine, you did for me.'"

Reflect:

These words from Jesus conclude his teaching on feeding the hungry, visiting the prisoner, caring for the poor. What is Jesus asking us to do? How could you increase your opportunity to serve in this way?

Day 3

Philippians 2: 3-4

"Do nothing out of selfish ambition or vain conceit. Rather, in humility value others above yourselves, not looking to your own interests but each of you to the interests of the others."

Reflect:

Where are you most tempted to let “selfish ambition” control you? Maybe at work, school, or even in a sports league? How can you value others above yourself in that setting?

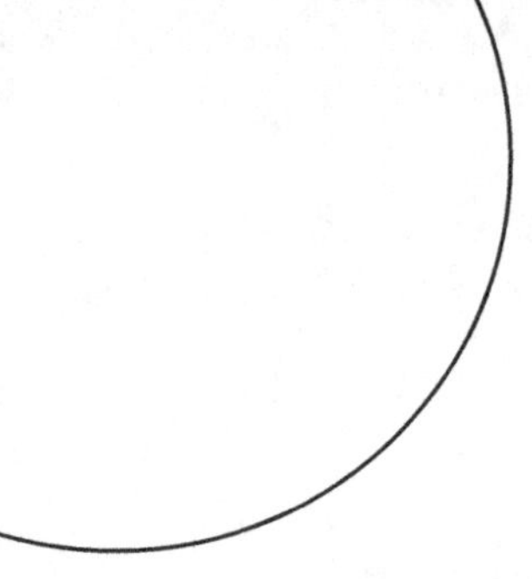

Day 4

Mark 10: 44-45

"...whoever wants to be first must be slave of all. For even the Son of Man did not come to be served, but to serve, and to give his life as a ransom for many."

Reflect:

What is one way you could follow Jesus' example of serving others today?

Day 5

Mark 9:35

"Sitting down, Jesus called the Twelve and said, 'Anyone who wants to be first must be the very last, and the servant of all.'"

Reflect:

In our competitive culture, it's hard to be willing to be last. What would that look like in your workplace? In your family?

Day 6

2 Corinthians 4:5

"For what we preach is not ourselves, but Jesus Christ as Lord, and ourselves as your servants for Jesus' sake."

Reflect:

What should our motive be for service, according to this verse? What does it mean to do something "for Jesus' sake?"

SESSION TWO

Discover Your God-Given Gifts

"In everything I did, I showed you that by this kind of hard work we must help the weak, remembering the words the Lord Jesus himself said: 'It is more blessed to give than to receive.'"

Acts 20:35

When we accept Christ and become part of God's family, the Bible tells us we each receive spiritual gifts—divine enablements that allow us to serve Christ's body, the church.

Whether you have a gift of encouragement, wisdom, teaching, helps, or something else, that gift is meant to be used! It may not make sense to you, but, when we use our gifts to serve, we experience joy and fulfillment. As we give, we receive—and others are blessed as well.

This week, we're going to talk about how we can discover and use our gifts to serve others.

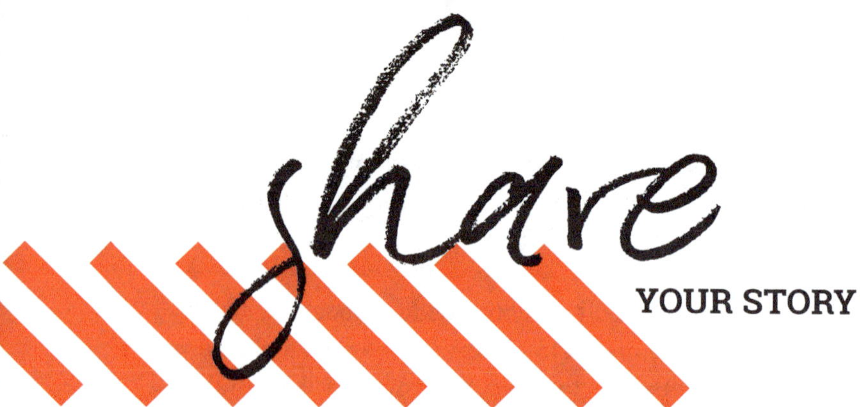

share YOUR STORY

Begin your time together by using the following questions to get the conversation started.

- If we describe a person as "gifted" at something, what does that mean?
- What did you learn from your daily devotions this week?

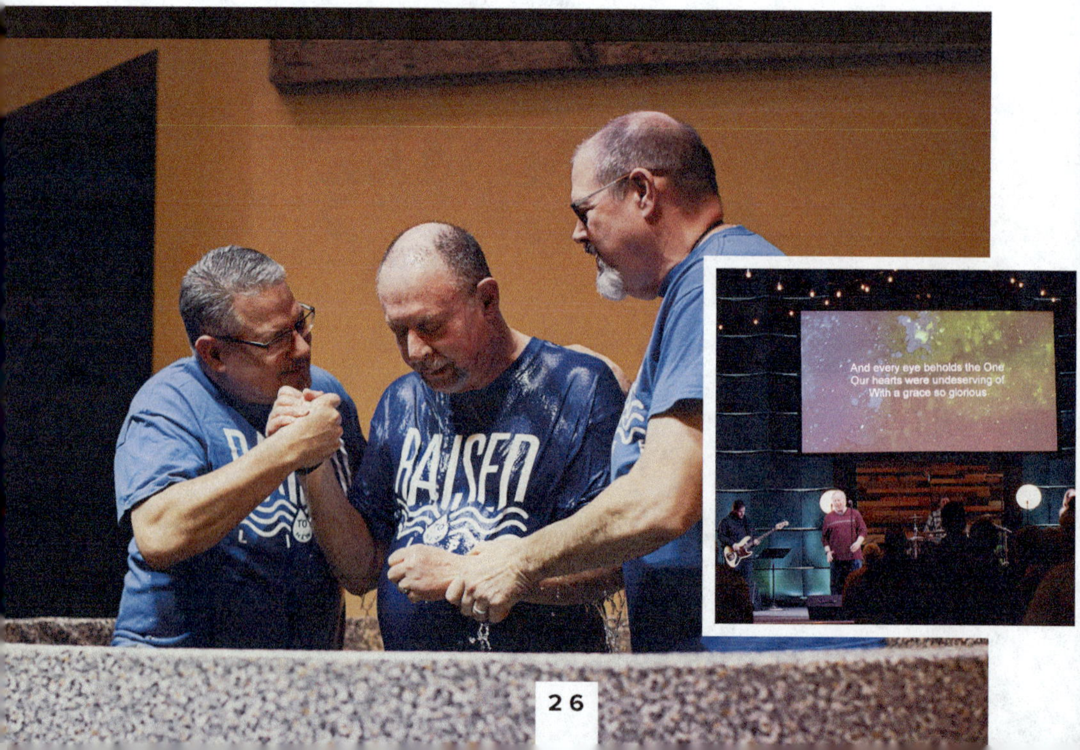

Restroo

watch THE VIDEO

Use the Notes space provided below to record your thoughts and questions as well as the things you want to remember or follow up on. After watching the video, have someone read the discussion questions in the Hear God's Story section and start the conversation.

EPIC

GOD'S STORY

Read Romans 12:4-8

"For just as each of us has one body with many members, and these members do not all have the same function, so in Christ we, though many, form one body, and each member belongs to all the others. We have different gifts, according to the grace given to each of us. If your gift is prophesying, then prophesy in accordance with your faith; if it is serving, then serve; if it is teaching, then teach; if it is to encourage, then give encouragement; if it is giving, then give generously; if it is to lead, do it diligently; if it is to show mercy, do it cheerfully."

- What do you think this text means when it says, “each member belongs to all the others?” In what ways do people belong to each other?
- How are gifts and grace related, according to this passage?
- Which spiritual gifts are listed in this passage? Do you know someone who has one of these gifts? Describe the way in which you see them using those gifts.

In this section, talk about how you will apply the wisdom you've learned from the teaching. Then think about practical steps you can take in the coming week to live out what you've learned.

In your workbook is a brief spiritual gifts assessment, which you heard about in the video.

Take some time right now to take this short assessment on page 72. Then share with each other the major themes you see for your giftedness or the major area where it seems clear that God has gifted you.

- How are you currently using your gifts to serve the body?
- How does your season of life impact where and whom you will serve?

Give each person an opportunity to share prayer requests. If you'd like, you can write these on the Prayer and Praise report on page 82.

Close your meeting with prayer.

Day 1

Acts 2:38

"Peter replied, 'Repent and be baptized, every one of you, in the name of Jesus Christ for the forgiveness of your sins. And you will receive the gift of the Holy Spirit.'"

Reflect:

Before we receive specific gifts from the Spirit, we receive the Spirit himself, which is a gift. What does this verse tell us we must do in order to receive this gift?

Day 2

1 Peter 4:10

"Each of you should use whatever gift you have received to serve others, as faithful stewards of God's grace in its various forms."

Reflect:

What gift (spiritual or material) have you received? How can you use that gift to serve others?

Day 3

Ephesians 4:2-3

"Be completely humble and gentle; be patient, bearing with one another in love. Make every effort to keep the unity of the Spirit through the bond of peace."

Reflect:

This passage assumes we will serve, and gives instruction on our attitude as we serve. How does God ask us to behave as we serve? What specific things can you to do "keep the unity of the Spirit"?

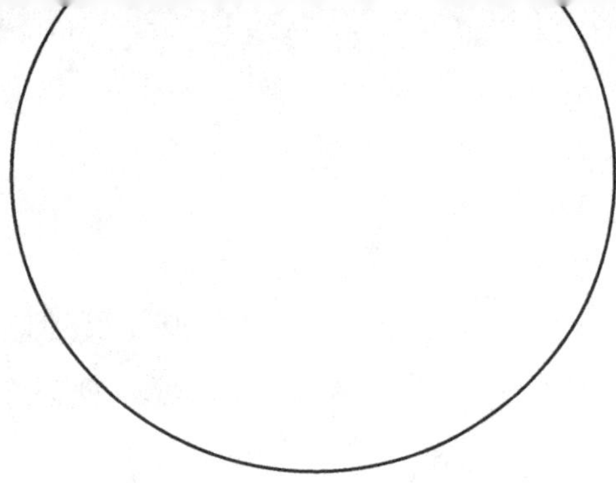

Day 4

Ephesians 4:11-12

"So Christ himself gave the apostles, the prophets, the evangelists, the pastors and teachers, to equip his people for works of service, so that the body of Christ may be built up."

Reflect:

Which gifts are mentioned here? What purpose do they have in common?

Day 5

Acts 9:36

"In Joppa there was a disciple named Tabitha (in Greek her name is Dorcas); she was always doing good and helping the poor."

Reflect:

Read more of Tabitha's story in Acts 9. What spiritual gifts do you think Tabitha had? How did her service impact the people around her?

Day 6

Ephesians 3:7-8

"I became a servant of this gospel by the gift of God's grace given me through the working of his power. Although I am less than the least of all the Lord's people, this grace was given me: to preach to the Gentiles the boundless riches of Christ..."

Reflect:

What attitude does Paul demonstrate through these words? What spiritual gift was he given?

SESSION THREE

Discover Your Gifts In Community

"Do nothing out of selfish ambition or vain conceit. Rather, in humility value others above yourselves, not looking to your own interests but each of you to the interests of the others."

Philippians 2: 3-4

We've each been given spiritual gifts—not for our own benefit, but the benefit of others. God intends that we use our gifts in community to build up the church.

When we read about gifts, we often find the word grace nearby in the text. Grace is a gift, and gifts are a way of extending and showing God's grace to others. Both are things we receive through no effort of our own, but because of God's love. And our gifts can be a wonderful way to extend God's grace to others.

In this session we're going to think and talk about what it means to serve others as part of God's family and to use our gifts in community.

YOUR STORY

Begin your time together by using the following questions to get the conversation started.

- Which of last week's Daily Devotions was particularly meaningful or encouraging to you? Explain.
- Tell about a time you felt welcomed into a group or community. What did people do to make you feel connected and welcomed?

THE VIDEO

Use the Notes space provided below to record your thoughts and questions as well as the things you want to remember or follow up on. After watching the video, have someone read the discussion questions in the Hear God's Story section and start the conversation.

GOD'S STORY

Read Philippians 2:3-8

"Do nothing out of selfish ambition or vain conceit. Rather, in humility value others above yourselves, not looking to your own interests but each of you to the interests of the others. In your relationships with one another, have the same mindset as Christ Jesus: Who, being in very nature God, did not consider equality with God something to be used to his own advantage; rather, he made himself nothing by taking the very nature of a servant, being made in human likeness. And being found in appearance as a man, he humbled himself by becoming obedient to death—even death on a cross!"

- In this passage, what words or phrases describe the steps Jesus took to move toward us and serve us? Underline them.

- What does this passage say our mindset should be?

- What does it mean to be “in very nature God?” What does it mean to take on “the very nature of a servant?”

In this section, talk about how you will apply the wisdom you've learned from the teaching. Then think about practical steps you can take in the coming week to live out what you've learned.

- In the text we read, it tells us to act like Jesus "in your relationships with one another." In which particular relationships do you find it challenging to act like Jesus?
- What is one way you could "value others above yourself" in your workplace or home in the coming week?
- What step of obedience do you sense God is currently inviting you to take?
- How can your group, as a small community, serve the larger community? What is a project your group could do together?

Give each person an opportunity to share prayer requests. If you'd like, you can write these on the Prayer and Praise report on page 82.

Close your meeting with prayer.

Day 1

1 Thessalonians 5:11
"Therefore encourage one another and build each other up, just as in fact you are doing."

Reflect:
What does this verse tell us about how we can serve others with our words? Who needs your encouragement this week?

Day 2

James 1:22
"Do not merely listen to the word, and so deceive yourselves. Do what it says."

Reflect:
What does this verse tell us about developing our gifts and growing in community and spiritual depth?

Day 3

James 5:16
"Therefore confess your sins to each other and pray for each other so that you may be healed. The prayer of a righteous person is powerful and effective."

Reflect:
According to this verse, what will result if we serve the body by praying for one another?

Day 4

Ephesians 4:29
"Do not let any unwholesome talk come out of your mouths, but only what is helpful for building others up according to their needs, that it may benefit those who listen."

Reflect:
How would choosing your words carefully serve others? How would it impact community?

Day 5

Ephesians 4:25
"Therefore each of you must put off falsehood and speak truthfully to your neighbor, for we are all members of one body."

Reflect:
In what ways, specifically, would "falsehood" injure the body of Christ? How would truthfulness strengthen community?

Day 6

Colossians 3:16
"Let the message of Christ dwell among you richly as you teach and admonish one another with all wisdom through psalms, hymns, and songs from the Spirit, singing to God with gratitude in your hearts."

Reflect:
What do you think it means to let Christ's message dwell among you? What practical ways does this verse suggest we could build community?

SESSION FOUR

Discover Your Place In God's Plan

"And we know that in all things God works for the good of those who love him, who have been called according to his purpose."

Romans 8:28

Have you ever been on a mission trip, or done a service project with a group from your church? While these experiences are wonderful and often life-changing, there's much more to service than just one-time events.

God calls us according to his purpose. He intends that we live a life of service to others—not just once in a while, but daily, as a lifestyle. Our attitude, as we learned last week, is to be like that of Jesus—always being willing to humbly serve others, whether that's in a specific role at church or just the way that we serve our families, co-workers, and friends.

When we understand our gifting and see our place in God's plan, service becomes a joyful opportunity instead of an obligation. Playing our part in God's redemptive plan is exciting and fulfilling. How can we do that? That's what we're going to discuss in this final session of our study.

share YOUR STORY

Begin your time together by using the following questions to get the conversation started.

- Which of last week's Daily Devotions was particularly meaningful to you? Explain.
- Tell about a time when you were so involved in a task or project that you lost track of time. What were you doing? What made it so engaging?

THE VIDEO

Use the Notes space provided below to record your thoughts and questions as well as the things you want to remember or follow up on. After watching the video, have someone read the discussion questions in the Hear God's Story section and start the conversation.

GOD'S STORY

Read Ephesians 2:6-10

"And God **raised** us up with Christ and **seated** us with him in the heavenly realms in Christ Jesus, in order that in the coming ages he might show the incomparable riches of his grace, expressed in his kindness to us in Christ Jesus. For it is by grace you have been saved, through faith—and this is not from yourselves, it is the gift of God—not by works, so that no one can boast. For we are God's handiwork, created in Christ Jesus to do good works, which God prepared in advance for us to do."

Read through this passage and underline the verbs—the action words (the first two are raised and seated). Who is the one taking most of the action in this passage—you or God?

- What do you think it means to be "saved by grace"? Explain how you understand the relationship between grace and works.

- Does our service earn God's favor or approval? If not, why do we serve?

- What do you think it means to be "God's handiwork?"

In this section, talk about how you will apply the wisdom you've learned from the teaching. Then think about practical steps you can take in the coming week to live out what you've learned.

- We're not saved by what we do, but we are called to do things. What, specifically, do you feel like God is calling you to do? What works has God created in advance for you to do?
- When God calls us, he equips us. What has God equipped you to do?
- What's a dream God has given you? What has become clearer about God's calling for your life?

Take some time as a group to affirm the gifts you see in one another. This can be a powerful exercise. Be sure that each person speaks, and each person receives affirmation. Members can say things like "I notice that you are always encouraging others, thank you for using that gift in our group," or "You always seem to be drawn to hurting people—perhaps you have the gift of mercy."

Give each person an opportunity to share prayer requests. If you'd like, you can write these on the Prayer and Praise Report on page 82.

Close your meeting with prayer.

Day 1

Ephesians 4:1

"As a prisoner for the Lord, then, I urge you to live a life worthy of the calling you have received."

Reflect:

What do you think it means to live a life worthy of your calling?

Day 2

1 Corinthians 1:26-27

"Brothers and sisters, think of what you were when you were called. Not many of you were wise by human standards; not many were influential; not many were of noble birth. But God chose the foolish things of the world to shame the wise; God chose the weak things of the world to shame the strong."

Reflect:

How has God used you, despite your weakness, to influence and impact people spiritually?

Day 3

James 2:26

"As the body without the spirit is dead, so faith without deeds is dead."

Reflect:

Once we've received salvation by grace, what do we need to do to keep our faith growing, alive and healthy?

Day 4

2 Thessalonians 1:11

"With this in mind, we constantly pray for you, that our God may make you worthy of his calling, and that by his power he may bring to fruition your every desire for goodness and your every deed prompted by faith."

Reflect:

How would you currently rate your "desire for goodness?" How many of your deeds are "prompted by faith?"

Day 5

1 Peter 2:9

"But you are a chosen people, a royal priesthood, a holy nation, God's special possession, that you may declare the praises of him who called you out of darkness into his wonderful light."

Reflect:

What does this verse tell us about the identity of every believer? What is our response to that identity to be?

Day 6

1 Peter 3:8

"Finally, all of you, be like-minded, be sympathetic, love one another, be compassionate and humble."

Reflect:

As we live out our calling in the body of Christ, what does this verse tell us we ought to value? How are we to act? Which of these values do you find difficult to live out?

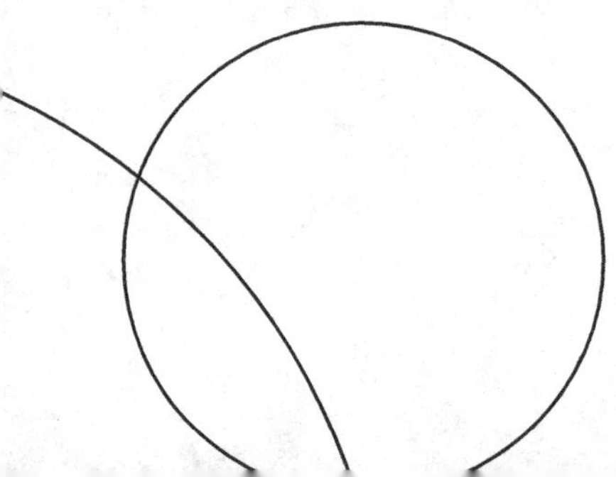

Appe

dices

What do we do on the first night of our group?
Like all fun things in life—have a party! A "get to know you" coffee, dinner, or dessert is a great way to launch a new study. You may want to review the Group Agreement (page 64) and share the names of a few friends you can invite to join you. But most importantly, have fun before your study time begins.

Can we do this study on our own?
Absolutely! This may sound crazy, but one of the best ways to do this study is not with a full house but with a few friends. You may choose to gather with another couple or a few friends who would enjoy going out for dinner and then walking through this study.

What if this group is not working for me?
You're not alone! This could be the result of a personality conflict, life stage difference, geographical distance, level of spiritual maturity, or any number of things. Relax. Pray for God's direction, and at the end of this study, decide whether to continue with this group or find another. However, don't bail out before the four weeks are up—God might have something to teach you. Also, don't run from conflict or prejudge people before you have given them a chance. God is still working in your life, too!

Who is the leader?
Most groups have an official leader. But ideally, the group will mature and members will rotate the leadership of meetings. Healthy groups often rotate hosts and leaders on a regular basis. This model ensures that all members grow, give their unique contribution, and develop their gifts.

How do we handle the childcare needs in our group?

Very carefully. Seriously, this can be a sensitive issue. We suggest that you empower the group to openly brainstorm solutions. You may try one option that works for a while and then adjust over time. One approach is for adults to meet in the living room or dining room and to share the cost of a babysitter (or two) who can watch the kids in a different part of the house. This way, parents don't have to be away from their children all evening when their children are too young to be left at home. A second option is to use one home for the kids and a second home (close by or a phone call away) for the adults. A third idea is to rotate the responsibility of providing a lesson or caring for the children. This can be an incredible blessing for kids. Finally, the most common solution is to decide that you need to have a night to invest in your spiritual lives individually or as a couple and to make your own arrangements for childcare. No matter what decision the group makes, the best approach is to dialogue openly about both the problem and the solution.

OUR PURPOSE

To provide an environment where participants experience authentic community and spiritual growth.

OUR VALUES

Group Attendance
To give priority to the group meeting. We will call or email if we will be late or absent. (Completing the Group Calendar on page 66 will minimize this issue.)

Safe Environment
To create a safe place where people can be heard and feel loved. (Please, no quick answers, snap judgments, or simple fixes.)

Respect Differences
To be gentle and gracious to fellow group members with different spiritual maturity, personal opinions, temperaments, or "imperfections." We are all works in progress.

Confidentiality
To keep anything that is shared strictly confidential and within the group, and to avoid sharing improper information about those outside the group.

Encouragement for Growth
To be not just takers but givers of life. We want to spiritually multiply our life by serving others with our God-given gifts.

Shared Ownership

To remember that every member is a minister and to ensure that each attender will share a small team role or responsibility over time.

Rotating Hosts/Leaders and Homes

To encourage different people to host the group in their homes and to rotate the responsibility of facilitating each meeting. (See the Group Calendar on page 66.)

OUR REMINDERS

Refreshments/mealtimes ....

Childcare ....

When we will meet (day of week) ....

Where we will meet (place) ....

We will begin at (time) .... and end at ....

We will do our best to have some or all of us attend a worship service together. Our primary worship service time will be ....

Date of this agreement ....

Date we will review this agreement again ....

Who (other than the leader) will review this agreement?

....

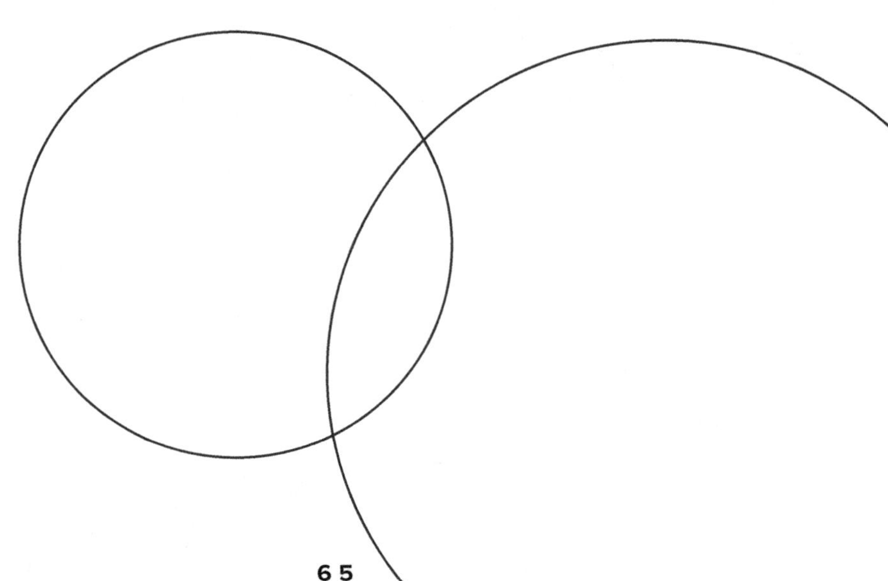

GROUP CALENDAR

MEETING DATE	LESSON NUMBER	HOST HOME	DESSERT/ MEAL	GROUP LEADER
Monday Jan. 15	1	Steve & Laura's	Joe	Bill

CLIP & REVIEW THE MEMORY VERSES ON THE OTHER SIDE OF THIS PAGE.

"...whoever wants to become great among you must be your servant, and whoever wants to be first must be your slave—just as the Son of Man did not come to be served, but to serve, and to give his life as a ransom for many."

Matthew 20:26-28

Two

"In everything I did, I showed you that by this kind of hard work we must help the weak, remembering the words the Lord Jesus himself said: 'It is more blessed to give than to receive.'"

Acts 20:35

Three

"Do nothing out of selfish ambition or vain conceit. Rather, in humility value others above yourselves, not looking to your own interests but each of you to the interests of the others."

Philippians 2: 3-4

Four

"And we know that in all things God works for the good of those who love him, who have been called according to his purpose."

Romans 8:28

DREAM
TEAM

God equips us each with powerful ministry tools. Discovering yours will help you find your place as a vital minister to your small group. Below are two tools to help you identify your shape for ministry. Use the first tool to begin the process. Take a few minutes to pray through each area and identify what you see as your strengths, interests, familiar experiences, temperament, and strenths. Then go to the next page and add your responses to the grid in the first column. In your group meeting you can ask your group to help you fill in the second column with their observations of what they see in you. Then after your group meeting you can pray through filling in the third column for what could be next for you!

GIFTS

Below you'll see a list of gifts, interests, experiences, temperaments, and strengths. Check all that apply to you.

- [ ] Preaching (1 Cor. 14:3)
- [ ] Evangelism (Acts 8:26-40)
- [ ] Discernment (1 John 4:1)
- [ ] Apostle (Rom. 15:20)
- [ ] Teaching (Eph. 4:12-13)
- [x] Encouragement (Acts 14:22)
- [ ] Wisdom (1 Cor. 2:1, 6-16)
- [x] Missions (1 Cor. 9:19-23, Acts 13: 2-3)
- [x] Service (Acts 6:1-7, 1 Cor. 12:28)
- [ ] Mercy (Rom. 12:8)
- [ ] Hospitality (1 Pe. 4:9-10)
- [ ] Pastoring (1 Pe. 5:2-4)
- [x] Giving (2 Cor. 8:1-7)
- [ ] Intercession (Col. 1:9-12)
- [x] Music (Ps. 150)
- [ ] Arts & Crafts (Exod. 31:3-11)
- [ ] Healing (Jas. 5:14-16)
- [ ] Miracles (Mark 11:23-24)
- [ ] Leadership (Heb. 13:7, 17)
- [ ] Administration (1 Cor. 14:40)
- [ ] Faith (Rom. 4:18-21)

INTERESTS

The people I would like to serve most are:

- ☒ Children
- ☒ Homeless
- ☐ Single Parents
- ☐ College Students
- ☐ Hospitalized
- ☐ Singles
- ☒ Youth
- ☒ Disabled
- ☒ Infants
- ☒ Teen Moms
- ☒ Poor
- ☐ Divorced
- ☐ Men
- ☐ Unemployed
- ☐ Elderly Parents
- ☐ Widowed
- ☐ Empty Nesters
- ☐ Prisoners
- ☒ Women

The issues or causes I feel most strongly about are:

- ☒ Abuse/Violence
- ☐ Drug Abuse
- ☐ Homelessness
- ☐ Sanctity of Life
- ☐ Alcoholism
- ☐ Education
- ☒ Injustice issues
- ☐ Sexuality yes! but no
- ☐ At-risk children
- ☒ Environment Law/ Justice system
- ☐ Spiritual apathy
- ☐ Compulsive behavior
- ☐ Ethics
- ☐ Marriage/Family
- ☐ Deafness
- ☐ Finances
- ☐ Parenting
- ☒ Disabilities
- ☐ Health/fitness
- ☐ Policy/Politics
- ☐ Divorce
- ☐ HIV/AIDS
- ☒ Poverty/Hunger

FAMILIAR EXPERIENCES

Think about the following experiences in your life:

- ☐ Spiritual experiences: meaningful decisions, times with God, times you felt especially close to God.
- ☐ Painful experiences: problems, hurts, trials, etc...
- ☐ Educational experiences: favorite subjects in school, special training, etc...
- ☐ Ministry experience: how you've served in the past.

TEMPERMENT

Extroverted	☐	☐	☒	Introverted
Self-controlled	☐	☒	☐	Self-expressive
Routine	☐	☒	☐	Variety
Cooperative	☐	☒	☐	Competitive

STRENGTHS

- [x] Adapting – The ability to adjust, change, alter, modify.
- [ ] Administering – The ability to govern, run, rule.
- [ ] Analyzing – The ability to examine, investigate, probe, evaluate.
- [ ] Building – The ability to construct, make, assemble.
- [ ] Coaching – The ability to prepare, instruct, train, equip, develop.
- [x] Communicating – The ability to share, convey, impart.
- [ ] Competing – The ability to contend, win, battle.
- [ ] Computing – The ability to add, estimate, total, calculate.
- [x] Connecting – The ability to link together, involve, relate.
- [ ] Consulting – The ability to advise, discuss, confer.
- [ ] Cooking – The ability to prepare, serve, feed, cater.
- [ ] Coordination – The ability to organize, match, harmonize.
- [ ] Counseling – The ability to guide, advise, support, listen, care for.
- [ ] Decorating – The ability to beautify, enhance, adorn.
- [ ] Designing – The ability to draw, create, picture, outline.
- [ ] Developing – The ability to expand, grow, advance, increase.
- [ ] Directing – The ability to aim, oversee, manage, supervise.
- [ ] Editing – The ability to correct, amend, alter, improve.
- [ ] Encouraging – The ability to cheer, inspire, support.
- [ ] Engineering – The ability to construct, design, plan.
- [ ] Excelling – the ability to be the best and make my team the best, setting and attaining the highest standard.
- [ ] Facilitating – The ability to help, aid, assist, make possible.
- [ ] Forecasting – The ability to predict, calculate, see trends, patterns, and themes.
- [ ] Implementing – The ability to apply, execute, make happen.
- [ ] Improving – The ability to better, enhance, further, enrich.
- [ ] Influencing – The ability to affect, sway, shape, change.
- [ ] Landscaping – The ability to garden, plant, improve.
- [ ] Leading – The ability to pave the way, direct, excel, win.
- [x] Learning – The ability to study, gather, understand, improve, expand self.
- [ ] Managing – The ability to run, handle, oversee.
- [ ] Mentoring – The ability to advise, guide, teach.
- [ ] Motivating – The ability to provoke, induce, prompt.
- [ ] Negotiating – The ability to discuss, consult, settle.

- [ ] Operating – The ability to run mechanical or technical things.
- [ ] Organizing – The ability to simplify, arrange, fix, classify, coordinate.
- [ ] Performing – The ability to sing, speak, dance, play an instrument, act out.
- [ ] Persevering – The ability to see things to completion, persisting at something until it is finished.
- [ ] Pioneering – The ability to bring about something new, groundbreaking, original.
- [ ] Planning – The ability to arrange, map out, prepare.
- [ ] Promoting – The ability to sell, sponsor, endorse, showcase.
- [ ] Recruiting – The ability to draft, enlist, hire, engage.
- [ ] Repairing – The ability to fix, mend, restore, heal.
- [ ] Researching – The ability to seek, gather, examine, study.
- [ ] Resourcing – The ability to furnish, provide, deliver.
- [x] Serving – The ability to help, assist, fulfill.
- [x] Shopping – The ability to collect, or obtain things, getting the highest quality for the best price.
- [ ] Strategizing – The ability to think ahead, calculate, scheme.
- [ ] Teaching – The ability to interpret, decode, explain, speak.
- [x] Traveling – The ability to journey, visit, explore.
- [x] Visualizing – The ability to picture, imagine, envision, dream, conceptualize.
- [ ] Welcoming – The ability to entertain, greet, embrace, make comfortable.
- [x] Writing – The ability to compose, create, record.

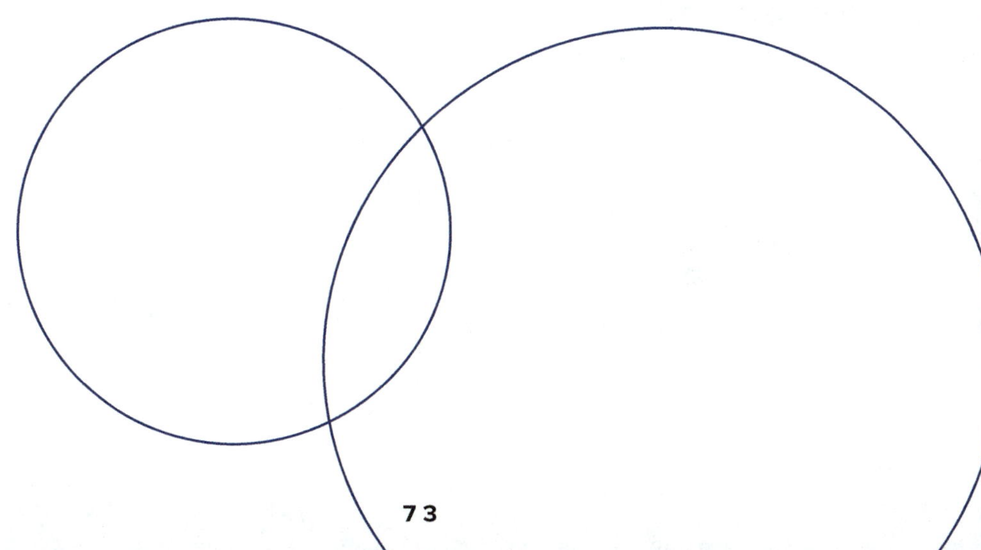

YOUR GIFTS	HOW DO I SEE MYSELF?	WHAT DO OTHERS SEE?	WHAT COULD BE NEXT?
GIFTS (SPIRITUAL)			
INTERESTS (PASSION)			
FAMILIAR EXPERIENCES			
TEMPERMENT (PERSONALITY)			
STRENGTHS (TALENTS)			

Small Grou

Leaders

AN OPEN HOUSE

If you're starting a new group, try planning an "open house" before your first formal group meeting. Even if you have only two to four core members, it's a great way to break the ice and to consider prayerfully who else might be open to joining you over the next few weeks. You can also use this kick-off meeting to hand out study guides, spend some time getting to know each other, discuss each person's expectations for the group and briefly pray for each other. A simple meal or good dessert always make a kick-off meeting more fun.

After people introduce themselves, have everyone respond to a few icebreaker questions:

- What is your favorite family vacation?
- What is one thing you love about your church/our community?
- What are three things about your life growing up that most people here don't know?

Next, ask everyone to tell what he or she hopes to get out of the study. You might want to review the Small Group Agreement and talk about each person's expectations and priorities.

Finally, set an open chair (maybe two) in the center of your group and explain that it represents someone who would enjoy or benefit from this group but who isn't here yet. Ask people to pray about inviting someone to join the group over the next few weeks. Hand out postcards and have everyone write an invitation or two. Don't worry about ending up with too many people; you can always have one discussion circle in the living room and another in the dining room after you watch the lesson. Each group could then report prayer requests and progress at the end of the session.

You can skip this kick-off meeting if your time is limited, but you'll experience a huge benefit if you take the time to connect with each other in this way.

Sweaty palms are a healthy sign.
The Bible says God is gracious to the humble. Remember who is in control. The time to worry is when you're not worried. Those who are soft in heart (and sweaty-palmed) are those whom God is sure to speak through.

Seek support.
Ask your leader, co-leader, or close friend to pray for you and prepare with you before the session. Walking through the study will help you anticipate potentially difficult questions and discussion topics.

Bring your uniqueness to the study.
Lean into who you are and how God wants you to uniquely lead the study.

Prepare. Go through the session material.
If you are using the video, listen to the teaching segment. Don't wait until the last minute to prepare.

Be time conscious.
Everyone leads busy lives. One of the greatest ways you can value people is by placing value on their time. Therefore, you will want to be certain you are beginning on time and concluding on time. Be aware of the clock throughout the group session.

Ask for feedback so you can grow.
Perhaps in an email or on cards handed out at the study, have everyone

write down three things you did well and one thing you could improve on. Demonstrate an openness to learn and grow.

Prayerfully consider launching a new group.
This doesn't need to happen overnight, but keep growth as a goal. Not all Christians are called to be leaders or teachers, but we are all called to be "shepherds" of a few someday.

Share with your group what God is doing in your heart.
God is searching for those whose hearts are fully His. Share your trials and victories. We promise that people will relate.

Prayer AND PRAISE REPORT

	PRAYER REQUEST	PRAISE REPORT
SESSION 1		
SESSION 2		
SESSION 3		
SESSION 4		

$10
GOOD
NEWS
IS COMING

small GROUP ROSTER

NAME	EMAIL	PHONE #

NAME	EMAIL	PHONE #